The Lost Hat Before
CHRISTMAS

Imagined and Illustrated by Eren, Age 6
Written by Eren´s Mom

For Lia and Jona from Switzerland – Eren

A special thanks to my friend, Lesley – Eren's Mom

"The Lost Hat Before Christmas" is
Imagined and Illustrated by Eren, Age 6
Written by Eren´s Mom
Edited by Ilker Hadzhalaran

Like us on Facebook: Eren and Mom
Visit us at www.erenandmom.com
Contact us at erenandmom@gmail.com

Designed by Creative Ivy Designs Inc.
www.creativeivydesigns.com

ISBN 978-1-928126-05-8

Dear Readers,

I wrote this story for a nice family we met at Eren's school. Their younger daughter, Jona, lost her hat at a Santa Claus parade and that inspired me to write this little Christmas story. Enjoy reading!

Eren's Mom

It was September when Lia and Jona arrived in Canada with their family, all the way from faraway Switzerland.

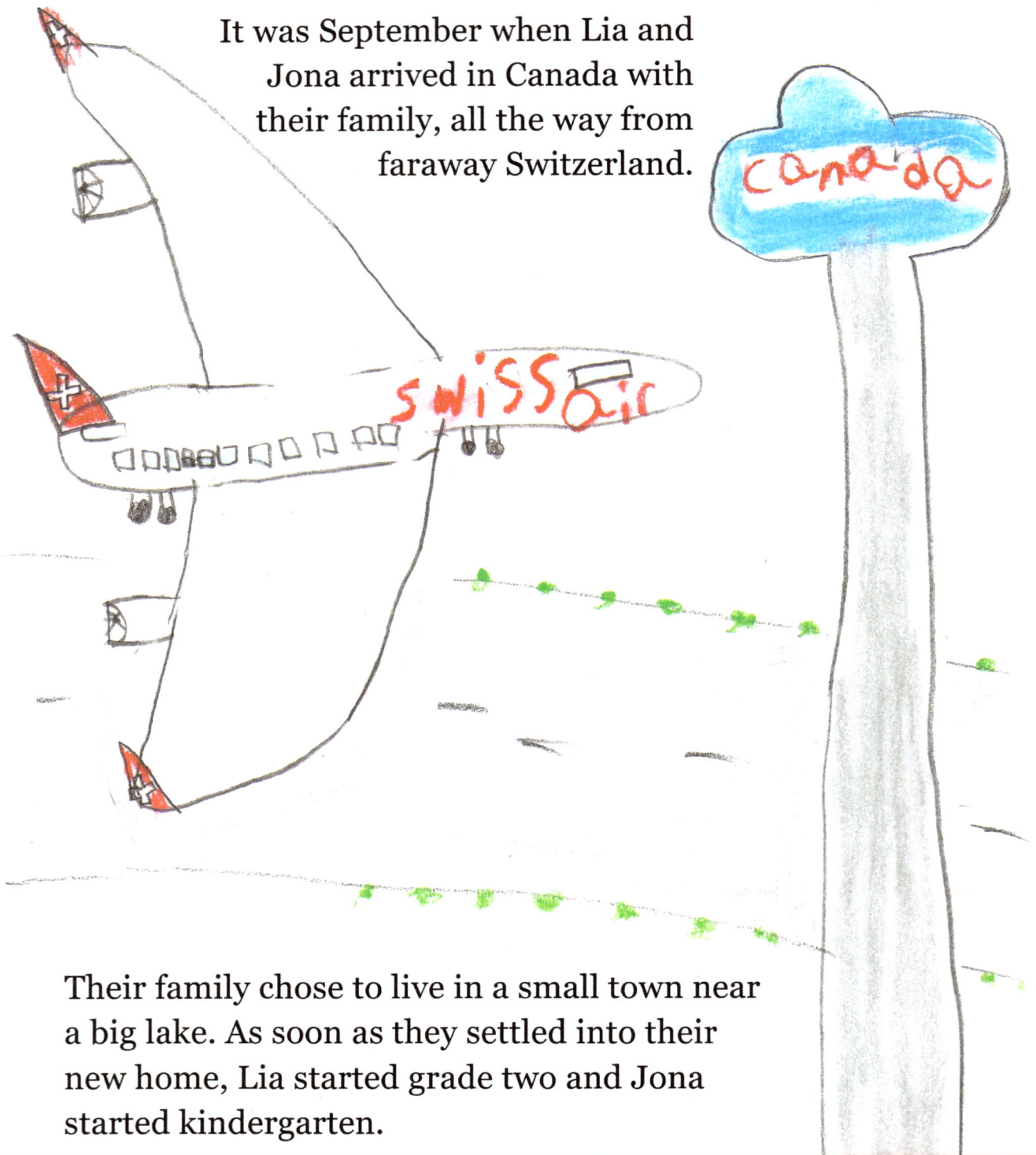

Their family chose to live in a small town near a big lake. As soon as they settled into their new home, Lia started grade two and Jona started kindergarten.

But, there was a problem - Jona, the younger sister, still missed her Switzerland.

One day, Jona's mom read in a newspaper,

"Santa Claus parade on Saturday."

Then she turned and asked, "Jona! Lia! Santa Claus is coming to town. Would you like to go and see him?"

"Hooray, Santa is coming to town!" the girls cheered, jumping up and down excitedly.

Early that Saturday morning, Lia and Jona were waiting for the parade to start. They were standing on the sidewalk of the town's main street. Soon Santa arrived and Jona asked loudly,
"Santa, please say 'Hello' to my grannies. They live in Switzerland."

Santa smiled and winked at Jona, "HO-Ho-Ho, sure thing dear, I will visit them tonight!"

When the parade was over, the family walked to their car. Lia and Jona were carrying small gift bags full of candy canes.

Just as Jona was opening the car door, she remembered something. "Mama, where is my hat?"

"I don't know Jona, maybe you left it somewhere in the car before the parade," answered her mom.

But the hat wasn't anywhere in the car so Jona got very upset.

"Oh Mama!" cried Jona, "I think I lost my purple hat at the Santa parade."

"Don't be sad, Jona!" comforted her mother, "I'm sure we'll find it."

They hurried back to the place where they stood during the parade. But the hat wasn't there.

That night, Jona went to bed worrying about her missing hat. She looked at the dark sky where all the stars were twinkling, but she couldn't relax, "What if my hat gets lonely?" she thought before falling asleep.

Later that night, when Jona went to bed, her mom decided to write a secret email to Santa. She wrote,

"Dear Santa,

We came from Switzerland and my little daughter Jona had brought her favourite hat to our new home here in Canada. Unfortunately, at your parade we lost it, so Jona is very sad. Can you please help us find her hat? She'd be very happy if she got it back and would wear it all through the winter. I am also sending you a picture of the missing hat so you know what it looks like.

Thank you,

Jona's mom"

The next morning, when Mr. Santa woke up, the first thing he did was read all his emails. There were thousands of them, written by kids from all over the world.

"HO - HO – HOLY MOLY, this is going to take me a while," said Santa, smoothing his long moustache.

Finally, he got to reading Jona's mom's email.
"Oh no," sighed Santa, "A lost winter hat? That's no good!"

Then he called to one of his elves,
"Elf! Elf!" said Santa quickly, "There's a little girl who's lost her hat. You have to go look for it before Christmas."

"But, Mr. Santa, how? Where am I going to find it?" asked the elf, confused.

Then Santa explained to the elf what he should do. He gave him about ten instructions that the elf jotted down in his notepad.

He sat on one of Santa's reindeer and commanded, "Let's go to Canada! My mission is to find a lost purple hat."

The elf went to the place where the parade had been held and started inspecting corners, sidewalks, and garbage bins. He didn't find anything except one small scarf and pair of mittens.

When he got tired, he returned back to the North Pole.

"Mr. Claus, I couldn't find anything except this small scarf and pair of mittens. I looked everywhere but, there was nothing," said the elf, shrugging his shoulders.

"I can't believe you couldn't find it!" said Santa and frowned, "Christmas is almost here. We must do something and do it quick."

Santa went to his desk to think up a new idea.
He called his new elf assistant and said,
"Now, Elf, you must learn how to knit a hat!"

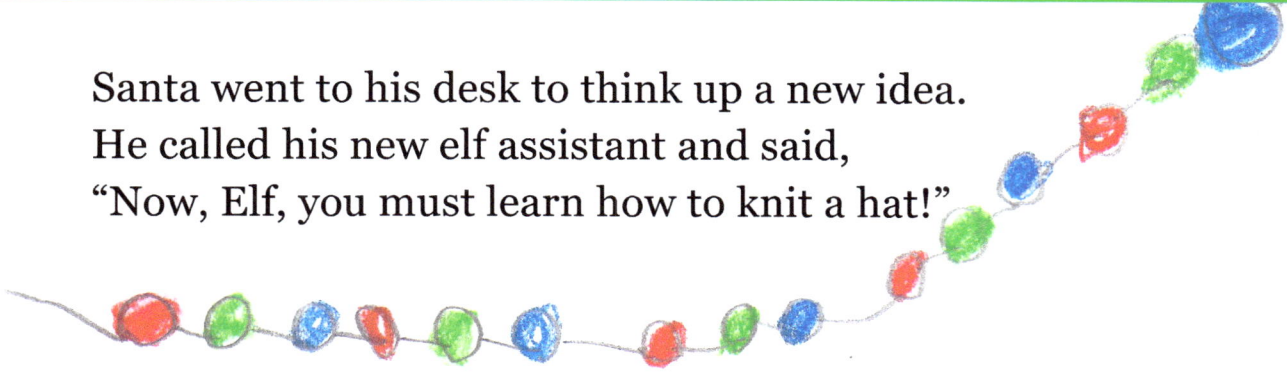

"What? A hat? But Santa," protested the elf, "I've never
knitted anything in my entire 364 year old life."

"Well it's never too late to learn a new skill," added Santa
and smiled, "I'm going to Germany
to buy the same yarns that
make up Jona's hat.
Ho-ho-ho,
now GO-GO-GO!"

After a few hours Santa returned from Germany with the knitting supplies: two knitting needles that were longer than the elf's arms and many balls of purple, green, gray, white, and black yarn. This elf meant business.

Santa gave him the picture of Jona's hat that Jona's mom had sent in her email. He ordered,
"You have three days to make the same hat. Please make sure to finish it before Christmas Eve!"

The elf murmured sourly, then after some grumbling, he started working with the yarn and the needles. At first it was very hard for him since the big knitting needles kept slipping out of his fingers and the balls of yarn kept tangling around his feet. He practiced again and again but he couldn't get it to work. It seemed nothing was going right for that poor Elf.

"Oh, my. What a difficult job it is to knit a hat!" groaned the elf, "I give up. No more knitting!"

But then, the elf remembered that Jona would be very sad
if she didn't get her hat back so he got an idea,
"Aha! Maybe I can go on YouTube to learn how to knit!"

He then turned on his computer, typed in
"S-T-E-P-S F-O-R K-N-I-T-T-I-N-G A H-A-T,"
and pressed the ENTER key.

The next morning, Jona woke up with a sad mood, "Mama," she called, "I don't know if I can go to school today."

"It's not that bad, Jona. It's just a hat," said Mama. But she knew it was more than just a hat for Jona.

This Christmas was different. So Mama decided to cheer Jona up by decorating the Christmas tree with many small hats.

It was one hour before midnight when Santa called, "Ho-Ho-Ho, time to deliver. Elves, please start loading up my sleigh."

"But, Santa, I'm not ready yet," called his assistant elf. "I'm not done knitting, I need more time!"

"I'll give you an hour," said Santa and ran outside, "I'm going to check on Rudolf."

While the elf was rushing to finish the hat he realized he had missed a stitch.

"Oh not now," sighed the elf, "I don't have time to fix it, I'll have to leave it as it is."

Next, he scurried to the wrapping area and wrapped the new hat with nice, purple wrapping paper, then put a large golden bow on it.

He wrote a card,

"A very special present for a very special girl."

—Santa's helper, Elf.

When Santa's sleigh was full of presents, he took off into the sky.

At midnight he went through Jona's chimney very quietly and left two packages under the Christmas tree. He ate a cookie and took a bite out of another. He also took a carrot for his reindeer, then he went to deliver presents to all the other good children of the world.

On Christmas morning, Jona and Lia woke up early and ran downstairs to see if Santa had paid them a visit. There, under the tree, Jona saw something wrapped in purple paper with a small card on it. When she opened her present she got a big surprise.

"Mama, Mama!" she called, "Santa found my hat!"

"I can't believe it!" answered her mom, "Santa must have been very busy looking for it."

So, in the end, the family ended up having a wonderful Christmas.

That winter, Jona wore her purple hat every single day but this time she was very careful not to lose it again. She loved it so much she didn't even notice the elf's missing stitch.

The end....

Other books by Eren and Eren's Mom:

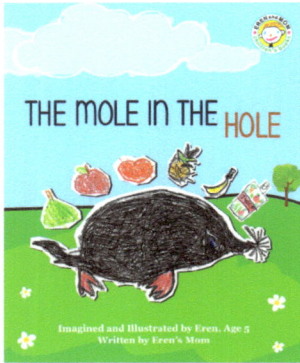

The Mole in the Hole

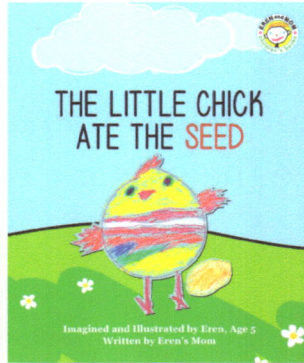

The Little Chick Ate the Seed

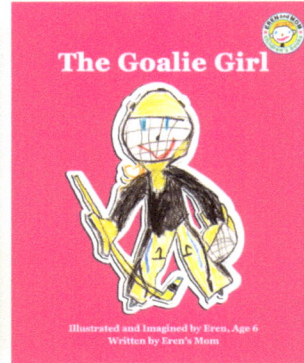

The Goalie Girl

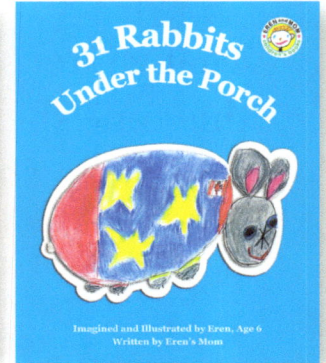

31 Rabbits Under the Porch

Take an adventurous journey to Space with The Boy Named Why series!

The Boy Named Why

Why and What Travel to Space

Why's Sunny Vacation

Why Meets Space Friends

Look out for books in The Sally Troublemaker series:

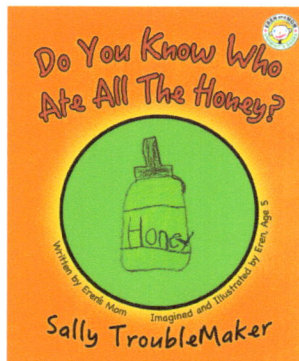

Do You Know Who Ate All the Honey?

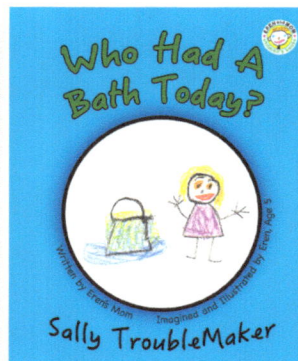

Who Had a Bath Today?

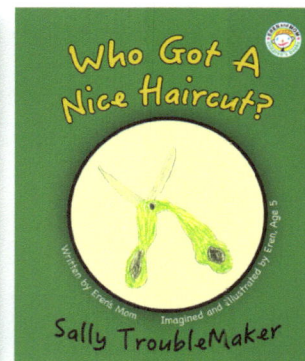

Who Got a Nice Haircut?

www.ingramcontent.com/pod-product-compliance
Lightning Source LLC
Chambersburg PA
CBHW060816090426
42737CB00002B/82